Whisk eggs & MILK

French Toast

Stacked | Stuffed | Baked

Donna Kelly

Photographs by Zac Williams

GIBBS SMITH
TO ENRICH AND INSPIRE HUMANKIND

This book is lovingly dedicated to families everywhere and to the tradition of sharing delicious meals—whether breakfast, lunch, or dinner, in unity and love.

23 22 21 20 19 5 4 3 2 1

Published by
Gibbs Smith
P.O. Box 667
Layton, Utah 84041

1.800.835.4993 orders
www.gibbs-smith.com

Designed by Sheryl Dickert
Printed and bound in China

Gibbs Smith books are printed on either recycled, 100% post-consumer waste, FSC-certified papers or on paper produced from sustainable PEFC-certified forest/controlled wood source. Learn more at www.pefc.org.

Library of Congress Cataloging-in-Publication Data

Names: Kelly, Donna, 1955- author.
Title: French toast: stacked, stuffed, baked / Donna Kelly.
Description: First edition. | Layton, Utah : Gibbs Smith, [2019] | Includes
bibliographical references and index.
Identifiers: LCCN 2018033193 | ISBN 9781423651352 (jacketless hardcover :
alk. paper)
Subjects: LCSH: French toast. | LCGFT: Cookbooks.
Classification: LCC TX770.F73 K45 2019 | DDC 641.81/5--dc23
LC record available at https://lccn.loc.gov/2018033193

contents

acknowledgments

This book is published with thanks to the many taste testers who frequent my home and provide frank and helpful critiques of my culinary experiments. I am most grateful to my daughter Kate; my daughter Amy and her sweet husband Chris; my sons Jake and Matt and their entourages always eager to sample my foods; my daughter Anne, for her culinary and other advice; and most of all my eternal companion Jim, the most patient and supportive husband on the planet. And to my granddarlings Lily, Charlotte, Ruby, and Coleman, for bringing joy into my life!

all about french toast

French toast is one of the oldest and most popular breakfast foods. It is derived from the original French recipe *pain perdu*, or "lost bread." It started as an ingenious way to use stale or "lost" bread by dipping it in an egg and milk mixture and cooking it. The concept lends itself to an almost infinite variety of flavors and versions—all easy enough to make even the average cook an instant gourmet.

Because French toast is so easy and convenient, I became its biggest fan when my children were small. As time went by, it became a family favorite and eventually crept into our family fare at meals other than breakfast. I found that, with a little experimenting, the possibilities with French toast were endless. Different types of breads opened up whole new worlds of flavors and combinations. Some of the most delicious mingled tastes were not the standard French toast with maple syrup, but rather a savory blend of cheeses, onion, and bits of meat. It was almost like a simplified and fail-safe version of a soufflé. Now French toast forms the base for many hearty and flavorful meals at our table, and I hope it does at your table too.

Breads

The term "day-old" is used throughout this book and is commonly used in the cooking world to mean bread that is dried out. This is important in French toast recipes, as fresh bread becomes too soggy and falls apart while cooking. Dry bread absorbs the egg and milk mixture better than fresh bread, which is what makes the classic French toast texture.

The best method for drying fresh bread is to set slices on a wire rack and then leave them out for several hours or overnight so that air can circulate around both sides of the bread. In a pinch, bread can be dried out in the oven by placing the slices directly on the oven racks and baking for 20 minutes at 200 degrees. You can also toast bread in a toaster for several seconds, watching closely so bread does not brown.

Generally, the quality of the bread determines the quality of the French toast recipe. Try specialty breads baked in local bakeries. Cinnamon swirls, cheese-topped, and other breads with added flavors will add character to your French toast recipes.

Cooking

Try experimenting with the quantity of eggs and milk for dipping the bread and find the proportions you like best. The general rule is 3 large eggs to 1 cup of milk. The standard proportion can be varied, depending on the individual recipe, but the more eggs you use, the denser and more custard-like the texture will be. Also, avoid adding large amounts of sugar to the egg mixture, as it will burn when cooking the French toast in a frying pan.

Classic French toast must be cooked one slice at a time, or in a pan big enough so that multiple slices don't touch while cooking. It works best to use a nonstick sauté pan, but to make sure the toast doesn't stick, spray the pan with a little nonstick cooking spray before cooking each slice. And, generally, the pan should be covered with a lid while cooking French toast to ensure that the middle is cooked through. To keep individual slices warm, place them on a wire rack on a baking sheet in a warm oven. Or, toast the slices lightly in a toaster just before serving to reheat.

When cooking French toast casseroles, make sure they have soaked for several hours or overnight in the refrigerator before baking. This allows

the bread and egg mixture to infuse thoroughly and helps to develop a custard-like texture. To ensure even cooking, always bring casseroles to room temperature before baking, which takes about 30 minutes.

Garnishes

French toast, like pancakes or waffles, can be garnished to make a more stunning and delightful presentation. Try adding some of the following garnishes to make your French toast look gourmet!

- Diced, sliced, or whole fresh fruits make colorful and flavorful toppings. Using fruits in season will add that extra special taste and touch to your toast.
- Powdered sugar, when sprinkled through a sieve or a paper doily, makes a unique pattern and elegant garnish.
- Try garnishing sweet French toasts with your favorite chopped nuts or crushed cereals and a drizzle of syrup. The sweet taste combined with the crunchy texture is rich and delicious.
- For savory French toasts, a sprinkling of grated cheeses or minced parsley not only adds flavor, but also adds a pop of color. Adding minced or diced peppers, or thinly sliced or julienned green onions will complement southwest-style toasts.

Storing

Cooked French toast slices are easy to store. Individual slices should be cooled before placing in a ziplock bag, separated by a piece of wax paper. They can be stored in the refrigerator up to three or four days, or can be frozen up to two weeks. To reheat, simply preheat oven to 350 degrees and bake on a baking sheet for a few minutes, or toast in the toaster until heated through. Serve with syrup or your favorite toppings.

French toast casseroles are best eaten straight from the oven because they are sometimes difficult to store due to the large dish in which they are usually baked. However, they can be covered and refrigerated for up to three days and then reheated in the oven at 350 degrees. Warm until heated thoroughly and slightly crisp around the edges. Serve with syrup or your favorite toppings.

Many recipes can be made ahead of time and stored in the refrigerator until ready to use. Just remove from the refrigerator about 30 minutes before baking and bring to room temperature—this helps it to bake evenly.

Creating Your Own French Toast Recipes

Once you have experimented with the recipes in this book, you will be ready to create your own French toast favorites. Try using cooked savory French toast slices as a base for your favorite cooked vegetables or meats and sauces. Bake casseroles using soaked French bread cubes tossed with your family's favorite foods. Use fruit breads and slices of dense cakes to form a base for decadent desserts with sweet toppings. Be bold and use new spices and flavorings with plain breads to give your toast an appetizing twist. And always remember, the possibilities are endless!

family favorites

chocolate hazelnut banana french toast

MAKES 4 SANDWICHES

Bananas and chocolate hazelnut spread are a match made in heaven—and the perfect decadent filling.

- 4 tablespoons cream cheese, softened, divided
- 8 slices day-old firm, thin white bread
- 1 banana, cut into 1/4-inch-thick slices
- 8 tablespoons chocolate hazelnut spread, divided
- 1 cup milk
- 1/4 cup flour
- 3 large eggs
- 2 teaspoons vanilla
- 1/2 teaspoon salt
- Butter
- Powdered sugar
- Toppings, of choice, optional

Spread 1 tablespoon of cream cheese on 1 side of 4 bread slices. Arrange banana slices over cream cheese, covering entirely. Spread 2 tablespoons of chocolate spread evenly over each remaining bread slice and place over top of bananas, with the chocolate side down.

In a pie plate or other shallow pan, whisk together the milk and flour until smooth; whisk in eggs, vanilla, and salt. Soak each of the sandwiches in egg mixture for 10–20 seconds on each side, or until just soaked through.

Melt a little butter in a small frying pan over medium-high heat. Add 1 of the sandwiches to the pan, cover, and cook on each side for 2–3 minutes, or until lightly browned. Repeat with remaining sandwiches. Sprinkle with powdered sugar or toppings, as desired.

the classic MAKES 6 TOASTS

This basic recipe can't be beat–moist and fluffy on the inside, crispy on the outside.

1 cup milk

¼ cup flour

3 large eggs

2 teaspoons vanilla

½ teaspoon salt

6 slices day-old firm white bread

Butter

Syrup, of choice

Old-Fashioned Buttermilk Syrup (page 122), optional

In a pie plate or other shallow pan, whisk together the milk and flour; whisk in eggs, vanilla, and salt. Soak bread slices in egg mixture for 10–20 seconds on each side, or until just soaked through.

Melt a little butter in a small frying pan over medium-high heat. Add 1 soaked bread slice to the pan, cover, and cook on each side for 2-3 minutes, or until lightly browned. Repeat with remaining bread slices. Serve with butter and syrup, as desired.

santa fe railroad MAKES 8 TOASTS

Served on the Santa Fe Railroad line in frontier America, this variation of the famous recipe combines two breakfast favorites–corn flakes and French toast–into one breakfast delight!

4 large eggs

2 cups milk

2 tablespoons vanilla

1/2 teaspoon salt

4 cups crushed corn flakes

2 tablespoons powdered sugar

1 teaspoon cinnamon

8 slices day-old firm white bread

Butter

Syrup, of choice

In a pie plate or other shallow pan, whisk together the eggs, milk, vanilla, and salt.

In a bowl, mix together the corn flakes, sugar, and cinnamon; spread mixture over a plate. Soak bread slices in egg mixture on each side for about 1 minute, and then press both sides of each slice into the corn flake mixture.

Melt a little butter in a small frying pan over medium heat. Add 1 coated bread slice to the pan, cover, and cook on each side for 2–3 minutes, or until lightly browned and crisp. Repeat with remaining bread slices. Serve with butter and syrup.

healthy start MAKES 6 TOASTS

The perfect marriage of healthy yogurt and flavorful fruit–a great way to start your day.

1 (6-ounce) container low-fat yogurt, any flavor

1/4 cup water

2 egg whites

6 slices day-old multigrain bread

3 teaspoons olive oil, divided

Fresh Fruit Purée (page 121), optional

Syrup, of choice, optional

If yogurt has large chunks of fruit, blend with the water in a blender, until smooth.

In a pie plate or other shallow pan, whisk together the yogurt, water, and egg whites. Dip bread slices in the yogurt mixture, covering completely, and let soak for 10–20 seconds on each side.

Heat 1/2 teaspoon oil in a small frying pan over medium-high heat. Add 1 soaked bread slice to the pan, cover, and cook on each side for 2–3 minutes, or until lightly browned. Repeat with remaining bread slices, adding 1/2 teaspoon oil to the pan each time. Serve with Fresh Fruit Purée or syrup, if desired.

waffle style MAKES 8 TOASTS

The combination of waffles and French toast creates a crispy crust that holds as much butter and syrup as your heart desires.

- 4 large eggs
- 1 cup milk
- 1 teaspoon vanilla
- 1 tablespoon sugar
- ½ teaspoon salt
- 8 (1-inch-thick) slices day-old challah or French bread
- Syrup, of choice, warmed
- Powdered sugar, optional
- Fresh fruit, of choice, optional

Preheat waffle iron according to manufacturer's directions, and spray generously with nonstick cooking spray.

In a pie plate or other shallow pan, whisk together the eggs, milk, vanilla, sugar, and salt. Soak bread slices one at a time in egg mixture on each side until completely soaked. Place a soaked slice in heated waffle iron, close lid, and cook until lightly brown. Repeat process, spraying iron with a little cooking spray before adding each slice of bread. Serve with syrup, powdered sugar, and/or fresh fruit.

elvis' favorite

MAKES 4 SANDWICHES

Elvis loved grilled peanut butter and banana sandwiches, so we're pretty sure this would be "the King's" breakfast of choice.

- 1 cup milk
- 3 large eggs
- ½ teaspoon salt
- 8 tablespoons creamy peanut butter
- 8 thin slices day-old firm white bread
- 1 large banana, mashed
- 4 teaspoons honey
- Butter
- Syrup, of choice, optional

In a pie plate or other shallow pan, whisk together the milk, eggs, and salt.

Spread 2 tablespoons of peanut butter evenly on 1 side of 4 bread slices and spread 1 side of remaining slices with ¼ of the mashed banana. Drizzle 1 teaspoon of honey over each banana topped slice.

Melt a little butter in a small frying pan over medium heat. Soak the dry side of 1 peanut butter-topped bread slice in the egg mixture for 10–20 seconds, or until soaked through. Place in the heated pan, peanut butter side up.

Soak the dry side of 1 banana-topped bread slice in egg mixture for 10–20 seconds, or until soaked through. Place banana side down on top of bread slice in the pan. Press with a spatula so the slices stick together. Cover, and cook on each side for 2–3 minutes, or until lightly browned. Serve sandwiches warm with syrup on the side for dipping, if desired.

surprise inside MAKES 6 SANDWICHES

These yummy breakfast sandwiches are filled with sweetened cream cheese!

4 large eggs

1/2 cup cream

1 tablespoon cinnamon

1/4 cup sugar

2 teaspoons vanilla, divided

1/2 teaspoon salt

12 thin slices day-old firm white bread

8 ounces cream cheese, softened

1 tablespoon pure maple syrup

Butter

Decadent Vanilla Cream Syrup (page 116)

In a bowl, whisk together eggs, cream, cinnamon, sugar, 1 teaspoon vanilla, and salt until frothy. Pour half of the egg mixture into a 9 x 13-inch pan. Lay 6 slices of bread over egg mixture in the pan, completely filling pan.

In a medium bowl, using a hand mixer, mix together the cream cheese, maple syrup, and 1 teaspoon vanilla. Place 2 heaping tablespoons of cream cheese mixture in the center of each bread slice in the pan. Top with remaining bread slices. Press firmly so that the cream cheese flattens slightly but doesn't ooze out. Pour remaining egg mixture evenly over the sandwiches and let soak for 10 minutes.

Melt a little butter in a small frying pan over medium-high heat. Using a wide spatula, remove 1 French toast sandwich from soaking pan and place in frying pan. Cover, and cook on each side for 2–3 minutes, or until lightly browned. Repeat with remaining sandwiches, melting a little butter in pan each time. Serve with Decadent Vanilla Cream Syrup drizzled over top.

crunchy graham dipping sticks MAKES 24 STICKS

The sweet crunchy graham cracker coating will appeal to everyone in your family, young and old alike.

- **6 slices Texas-style toast, or other firm, thick white bread, lightly toasted**
- **1 cup heavy cream**
- **2 large eggs**
- **1 teaspoon vanilla**
- **½ teaspoon salt**
- **9 whole graham crackers, crushed into fine crumbs**
- **Canola oil**
- **Syrup, of choice**

Cut each toasted bread slice lengthwise into 4 sticks.

In a pie plate or other shallow pan, mix together the cream, eggs, vanilla, and salt. Spread graham cracker crumbs on a plate. Heat a little oil in a small frying pan over medium heat.

Working in small batches, dip bread sticks, one at a time, into egg mixture and then press into cracker crumbs, coating completely. Add to pan, cover, and cook sticks on each side for 2–3 minutes, or until lightly browned. Cool until warm enough to handle. Serve with a side of syrup for dipping.

VARIATION: *Preheat oven to 425 degrees. Oil a large baking sheet and place all the coated bread sticks in a single layer on the sheet. Bake for 8 minutes. Turn sticks over and bake another 3 minutes.*

one-eyed bandit MAKES 6 TOASTS

Cook your eggs with your French toast in this twist on the classic favorite from the '50s.

1 cup milk
¼ cup flour
9 large eggs, divided
2 teaspoons vanilla
½ teaspoon salt
6 slices day-old firm white bread
Butter
Syrup, of choice

In a pie plate or other shallow pan, whisk together the milk and flour; whisk in 3 eggs, vanilla, and salt.

Cut a hole in the center of each bread slice using a 3-inch round cookie cutter. Soak 1 bread slice and the cut out piece of bread in the egg mixture for 10–20 seconds on each side, or until just soaked through.

Melt a little butter in a small frying pan over medium-high heat. Place soaked bread slice and cut out piece in the pan and crack 1 egg into the center hole. Cover, and cook the bread slice and circle on each side for 2–3 minutes, or until lightly browned, and egg is cooked to desired doneness. To serve, place the bread circle slightly off-center, just covering part of the egg and top with butter and syrup.

brunch time

eggs benedict stacks MAKES 4 SERVINGS

This easy but elegant twist on an old breakfast tradition looks and tastes gourmet.

6 large eggs, divided

$^2/_3$ cup milk

$^1/_4$ teaspoon salt

8 English muffins, split in half

Easy Blender Hollandaise Sauce (page 121)

8 slices Canadian bacon

In a pie plate or other shallow pan, whisk together 2 eggs, milk, and salt. Soak each of the muffin halves for 1–2 minutes on each side.

Heat a small frying pan sprayed with nonstick cooking spray over medium-high heat. Add 1 muffin half to the pan, cover, and cook on each side for about 2 minutes, or until lightly browned. Repeat.

Cook the remaining eggs individually as desired. To assemble stacks, toast 2 muffin halves for 1 minute, or until lightly crisp. Place 1 of the halves on an individual serving plate and spread 1 tablespoon of hollandaise sauce over top. Place 2 slices of bacon over sauce and top with a cooked egg; drizzle generously with more sauce and lay remaining muffin half over top.

chai latte MAKES 8 TOASTS

Try this modern café flavor in an updated French toast!

1 cup milk

3 tablespoons instant powdered chai latte drink mix

3 large eggs

8 (1-inch-thick) slices day-old challah or French bread

Butter

Syrup, of choice

In a pie plate or other shallow pan, whisk together the milk and latte powder; whisk in the eggs. Soak each bread slice for 10–20 seconds on each side, or until just soaked through.

Melt a little butter in a small frying pan over medium-low heat. Place 1 bread slice in the pan, cover, and cook on each side for 2–3 minutes, or until lightly browned. (The sugar in the powdered drink mix will burn if the pan is too hot, so watch the heat closely and lower as necessary while cooking.) Repeat with remaining bread slices. Serve with butter and syrup.

stuffed croissants MAKES 6 SANDWICHES

This is a delicious and easy recipe that is elegant enough to serve to company.

2 eggs

1 cup milk

2 teaspoons vanilla

12 medium-sized day-old croissants

8 ounces cream cheese, softened

1/4 cup powdered sugar, plus extra

1 pint strawberries, hulls removed and thinly sliced

Butter

Powdered sugar, optional

In a bowl, whisk together the eggs, milk, and vanilla; pour into a 9 x 13-inch baking pan.

Slice each croissant in half lengthwise, but do not cut completely through. In a medium bowl, using a hand mixer, mix together the cream cheese and 1/4 cup sugar. Spread a layer of cream cheese mixture on the cut sides of each croissant and cover one of the sides with strawberries; press lightly together. Soak each side of croissant in the egg mixture for 2–3 minutes.

Melt a little butter in a small frying pan over medium heat. Place 1 sandwich in pan, cover, and cook on each side for about 1 minute, or until lightly browned. Sprinkle with powdered sugar, if desired.

VARIATION: *Replace strawberries with any fruit, such as peaches, kiwis, or raspberries.*

orange sunshine MAKES 8 SANDWICHES

Forget drinking a glass of orange juice for breakfast; get your citrus fix with an orange and cheese-filled French toast sandwich.

- 1 cup orange sherbet, melted
- 4 large eggs
- 1/2 cup milk
- 8 ounces cream cheese, softened
- 2 tablespoons frozen orange juice concentrate
- 16 (1/2-inch-thick) slices day-old French bread
- 8 tablespoons orange marmalade
- Butter
- Citrus Sunshine Syrup (page 125)

In a pie plate or other shallow pan, whisk together the sherbet, eggs, and milk. In a small bowl, using a hand mixer, mix together the cream cheese and orange juice.

Spread 1 side of 8 bread slices with 1 tablespoon cream cheese mixture, and spread 1 tablespoon marmalade over top. Spread 1 side of remaining bread slices with 1 tablespoon cream cheese mixture. Melt a little butter in a small frying pan over medium heat.

Soak the dry side of 1 bread slice with the cream cheese and marmalade in egg mixture for about 30 seconds. Place in heated pan, soaked side down. Soak the dry side of 1 bread slice with just the cream cheese in egg mixture for about 30 seconds. Place on top of the slice in the pan, cream cheese side down. Cover, and cook each side for about 2 minutes, or until lightly browned. Repeat with remaining bread slices. Serve hot with Citrus Sunshine Syrup.

cinnamon craving MAKES 6 TOASTS

And you thought raisin bread couldn't get any yummier!

1 cup milk

1/4 cup flour

3 large eggs

2 teaspoons vanilla

1/2 teaspoon salt

1/2 teaspoon cinnamon

6 slices day-old cinnamon raisin bread

Butter

Cinnamon Cream Syrup (page 122)

In a pie plate or other shallow pan, whisk together the milk and flour; whisk in eggs, vanilla, salt, and cinnamon. Soak each bread slice for 10–20 seconds on each side, or until just soaked through.

Melt a little butter in a small frying pan over medium heat. Add 1 bread slice to the pan, cover, and cook for 1–2 minutes on each side, or until lightly browned. Repeat with remaining bread slices. Serve with butter and Cinnamon Cream Syrup.

dairy free MAKES 8 TOASTS

With tofu and soy milk, this recipe tastes great and is extra healthy!

½ cup soft tofu

1 cup vanilla soy milk

1 teaspoon vanilla

1 teaspoon cinnamon

¼ teaspoon turmeric

8 slices day-old dairy-free bread

Syrup, of choice

Toppings, of choice

Place the tofu, milk, vanilla, cinnamon, and turmeric in a blender, and blend until smooth; pour into a pie plate or other shallow pan. Dip bread slices one at a time in mixture for a few seconds on each side, soaking evenly.

Heat a small frying pan sprayed with nonstick cooking spray over medium heat. Add 1 bread slice to the pan, cover, and cook on each side for 2–3 minutes, or until lightly browned and firm. Repeat with remaining bread slices. Serve with syrup or toppings, as desired.

tropical paradise MAKES 8 TOASTS

What could taste more tropical than coconut, pineapple, and rum?

4 large eggs

1 (14-ounce) can coconut milk, shaken

½ cup apricot pineapple jam

1 teaspoon rum flavoring

4 cups corn flakes

1 cup chopped macadamia nuts

1 cup sweetened shredded coconut

8 slices day-old firm white bread

Butter

Syrup, of choice

In a blender, mix together the eggs, milk, jam, and rum; pour mixture into a pie plate or other shallow pan.

In a food processor, pulse together the corn flakes, nuts, and coconut until they resemble coarse crumbs; spread on a plate. Soak bread slices in egg mixture for about 1 minute on each side and then press into crumb mixture covering both sides.

Melt a little butter in a small frying pan over medium heat. Place 1 coated bread slice in the pan, cover, and cook on each side for 2–3 minutes, or until lightly browned and crisp. Repeat with remaining bread slices. Serve with butter and syrup.

IMPORTED

brie and apple stuffed MAKES 6 SANDWICHES

Try this gourmet combination of creamy Brie and crunchy apples for an extra flavorful brunch.

3 large eggs

1 cup milk

1 teaspoon vanilla

1/2 teaspoon salt

1/4 teaspoon cinnamon

1/8 teaspoon nutmeg

Butter

12 (1/2-inch-thick) slices day-old French bread

8 ounces Brie, thinly sliced (rind removed)

1 Golden Delicious apple, peeled and cut into 1/8-inch-thick slices

Syrup, of choice

In a pie plate or other shallow pan, whisk together the eggs, milk, vanilla, salt, cinnamon, and nutmeg.

Melt a little butter in a small frying pan over medium-high heat. Dip one side of 1 bread slice into egg mixture for about 30 seconds. Place soaked side down in the pan and top with Brie and apple slices. Dip a second slice of bread into egg mixture and place on top of the apples, soaked side up. Cover the pan and cook sandwich on each side for 2–3 minutes, or until lightly browned. Repeat with remaining sandwiches. Serve with butter and syrup.

banana supreme MAKES 4 SANDWICHES

Banana bread stuffed with a sweet almond cream and more bananas really hits the spot.

8 (1/2-inch-thick) slices day-old firm banana bread

4 tablespoons cream cheese, softened

1 teaspoon almond extract

2 tablespoons powdered sugar

1/2 cup sweetened condensed milk

3 eggs

1 teaspoon vanilla

2 ripe bananas, thinly sliced

Caramel syrup, optional

Syrup, of choice, optional

Spread bread slices out on a baking sheet to dry for a few hours or overnight, turning at least once.

In a small bowl, using a hand mixer, mix together the cream cheese, almond extract, and sugar. In a pie plate or other shallow pan, whisk together the milk, eggs, and vanilla.

Heat a small frying pan sprayed with nonstick cooking spray over medium heat. Soak 1 side of a bread slice in egg mixture for 10 seconds and place soaked side down in the pan. Spread 1/4 of the cream cheese mixture over top and lightly press 1/4 of the banana slices into cream cheese. Soak 1 side of another bread slice and place dry side down over bananas; press slightly to seal. Cover, and cook on each side for 1–2 minutes, or until lightly browned. Repeat with remaining sandwiches. Serve with a drizzle of caramel or syrup, as desired.

german style MAKES 8 TOASTS

Try this French toast version of the classic German oven pancake for something unique and flavorful.

3 large eggs, separated

1 cup milk

1/4 cup frozen lemonade concentrate, thawed

Zest of 1 lemon

1 teaspoon vanilla

1/2 teaspoon salt

2 cups unseasoned breadcrumbs, toasted

8 (1-inch-thick) slices day-old French bread

2 tablespoons butter

4 to 6 Granny Smith apples, peeled and thinly sliced

1 (8-ounce) jar caramel sauce

8 tablespoons cinnamon sugar

Preheat oven to 350 degrees. Prepare a baking sheet with nonstick cooking spray.

In a pie plate or other shallow pan, whisk together the egg yolks, milk, lemonade, zest, vanilla, and salt. In a small bowl, whisk the egg whites and place in a separate pie plate. Spread breadcrumbs on a plate. Dip both sides of each bread slice first in the egg mixture, then egg whites, and finally in breadcrumbs. Place on baking sheet and bake for 15 minutes; turn and bake 15 minutes more.

In the meantime, melt the butter in a large frying pan over medium heat and sauté apples until cooked through and lightly browned, about 10 minutes. Stir in caramel and turn off heat. Remove bread slices from oven and sprinkle with cinnamon sugar. Top with apples and caramel.

apple-nut stuffed sammies MAKES 4 SANDWICHES

This is a sure winner for an easy and delicious fruit-and-nut-stuffed breakfast treat.

8 ounces cream cheese, softened

2 tablespoons powdered sugar

½ teaspoon cinnamon

1 (21-ounce) can apple pie filling

1 teaspoon orange zest

½ cup chopped pecans or walnuts

¼ cup chopped raisins or dried cranberries

2 eggs

½ cup milk

¼ cup unsweetened applesauce

8 (1½-inch-thick) slices day-old French bread

In a small bowl, using a hand mixer, mix together the cream cheese, sugar, and cinnamon.

In a medium bowl, stir together the pie filling, zest, nuts, and raisins. In a pie plate or other shallow pan, whisk together the eggs, milk, and applesauce. Cut the bread slices almost in half and spread each half with 1 tablespoon cream cheese mixture. Spread ¼ cup apple mixture in the center and close bread, pressing slightly to seal. Dip both sides of bread in egg mixture.

Heat a small frying pan sprayed with nonstick cooking spray over medium heat. Place a filled bread slice in the pan, cover, and cook on each side for 2–3 minutes, or until lightly browned. Repeat with remaining bread slices and filling.

huevos rancheros stacks MAKES 6 SERVINGS

This South-of-the-Border breakfast is even better with a base of tortilla French toast. Olé!

3 large eggs

1 cup milk

1 teaspoon chipotle chile powder

½ teaspoon salt

12 (6-inch) flour tortillas

1 (16-ounce) can refried beans

3 cups grated cheddar cheese

1 (14-ounce) can red enchilada sauce

6 poached or fried eggs, cooked to desired doneness

In a pie plate or other shallow pan, whisk together the eggs, milk, chile powder, and salt.

Heat a small frying pan sprayed with nonstick cooking spray over medium-high heat. Dip a tortilla completely in the egg mixture, shaking off excess; add to the pan, and cook for 30 seconds on each side. Spread 1 tablespoon of egg mixture on cooked side of tortilla, flip, and cook for 30 seconds. Repeat this process with each tortilla until a layer of lightly browned egg coats each side.

Place 1 coated tortilla on a microwave-safe serving plate and spread 3 tablespoons of beans over top; sprinkle ¼ cup cheese over beans. Place another coated tortilla over the cheese and pour ¼ cup enchilada sauce over top, allowing to drizzle over the edges. Top with 1 egg and drizzle a little more sauce over egg; sprinkle with ¼ cup cheese. Microwave for 1 minute, or until cheese is melted and stack is heated through. Repeat with remaining tortillas.

raspberry cheesecake MAKES 6 SANDWICHES

The creamy raspberry center is so delicious you will wonder if this is breakfast or dessert!

- 3 large eggs
- 1 cup milk
- 1 teaspoon vanilla
- 1/2 teaspoon salt
- 12 (1/2-inch-thick) slices day-old French bread
- 8 ounces cheesecake-flavored whipped cream cheese*
- 6 tablespoons low-sugar raspberry jam
- Raspberry Syrup (page 118)

In a pie plate or other shallow pan, whisk together the eggs, milk, vanilla, and salt.

Spread 1 side of 6 bread slices with 1 tablespoon cream cheese. Spread 1 tablespoon jam on 1 side of remaining slices. Press 1 cream cheese and 1 jam slice together to form a sandwich; lightly sealing edges together. Dip both sides of sandwich in egg mixture.

Heat a small frying pan sprayed with nonstick cooking spray over medium heat. Add 1 sandwich to the pan, cover, and cook on each side for 2–3 minutes, or until lightly browned. Repeat with remaining bread slices. Serve with Raspberry Syrup.

*IF *cheesecake-flavored cream cheese is not available, use 8 ounces regular whipped cream cheese and stir in 2 tablespoons instant cheesecake pudding mix.*

celebrations

new year's day shrimp bites MAKES 24 APPETIZERS

These seafood appetizers will add a gourmet touch to your New Year's feast.

- 12 slices day-old dark pumpernickel bread
- 1 cup milk
- 2 tablespoons flour
- ½ teaspoon salt
- 3 large eggs
- Butter
- ½ cup whipped cream cheese
- 3 tablespoons basil and pine nut pesto
- 24 jumbo cooked-and-peeled deli shrimp, chilled

Using a 2 ½ to 3 inch cookie cutter (festive shapes preferred), cut 2 shapes from each slice of bread.

In a pie plate or other shallow pan, whisk together the milk, flour, and salt; whisk in eggs until completely blended. Dip bread pieces in egg mixture for a few seconds on each side, gently shaking away any excess.

Melt a little butter in a small frying pan over medium-high heat. Working in small batches, add coated bread pieces to the pan, cover, and cook on each side for 2–3 minutes, or until well browned and crisp. Place on wire racks to cool.

In a small bowl, mix together the cream cheese and pesto. Place 1 rounded teaspoonful of cream cheese mixture on each bread piece, making sure to use all the cream cheese mixture. Top each toast with 1 shrimp. Serve chilled.

cherry valentines

MAKES 4 SERVINGS

Wake your valentine with a sweet and creamy romantic breakfast.

1 cup heavy cream, whipped
¼ cup sugar
1 teaspoon vanilla
8 ounces whipped cream cheese
1 cup milk
3 large eggs
1 teaspoon almond extract
½ teaspoon salt
Few drops red food coloring, if desired
8 slices day-old firm white bread
Chunky Cherry Syrup (page 119)
Powdered sugar

In a medium bowl, using a hand mixer, mix together the whipped cream, sugar, vanilla, and cream cheese; chill.

In a pie plate or other shallow pan, whisk together the milk, eggs, almond extract, and salt. Add a few drops of food coloring to make the mixture pink, if desired. Cut a large heart out of each bread slice using a heart-shaped cookie cutter. Soak hearts one at a time in egg mixture for 10 seconds on each side.

Heat a small frying pan sprayed with nonstick spray over medium heat. Place 1 of the hearts in the pan, cover, and cook on each side for 2–3 minutes, or until lightly browned. Let cool to room temperature. Repeat with remaining bread hearts.

To serve, spread ¼ of the cream filling between 2 heart slices, place on an individual serving plate, and generously spoon syrup around the plate. Dust with powdered sugar.

harvest pumpkin spice MAKES 8 TOASTS

Warm up on a crisp fall day with this special French toast treat made with cinnamon, nutmeg, cream, and pumpkin bread.

1 cup heavy cream, whipped

1/4 cup sugar

1 teaspoon vanilla

8 ounces whipped cream cheese

1 teaspoon cinnamon, plus extra

1/2 teaspoon nutmeg, plus extra

3 large eggs

1 cup milk

1/2 teaspoon salt

8 (1/2-inch-thick) slices sturdy, day-old pumpkin bread

In a medium bowl, using a hand mixer, mix together the whipped cream, sugar, vanilla, cream cheese, 1 teaspoon cinnamon, and 1/2 teaspoon nutmeg; chill.

In a pie plate or other shallow pan, whisk together the eggs, milk, and salt. Soak bread slices in egg mixture for about 30 seconds on each side.

Heat a small frying pan sprayed with nonstick cooking spray over medium heat. Place 1 slice of soaked bread in the pan, cover, and cook on each side for 2–3 minutes, or until lightly browned. Let cool to slightly warm. Repeat with remaining bread slices.

Spread a thick layer of cream cheese mixture over each toast and sprinkle with cinnamon or nutmeg, as desired.

red, white, and blueberry stacks MAKES 8 SERVINGS

Top your patriotic breakfast stack with a little flag to make it extra special!

1 1/2 cups heavy cream, whipped

1/4 cup sugar

1 teaspoon vanilla

8 ounces whipped cream cheese

1 1/2 cups milk

4 large eggs

1 teaspoon vanilla

1/2 teaspoon salt

16 slices day-old firm white bread

4 cups fresh blueberries

4 cups diced strawberries

Powdered sugar, optional

Chunky Cherry Syrup (page 119) or Raspberry Syrup (page 118), optional

In a medium bowl, using a hand mixer, mix together the whipped cream, sugar, vanilla, and cream cheese; chill.

In a pie plate or other shallow pan, whisk together the milk, eggs, vanilla, and salt. Cut a large star out of each bread slice using a star-shaped cookie cutter. Soak the stars in egg mixture for 10 seconds on each side.

Heat a frying pan sprayed with nonstick cooking spray over medium heat. Place 1 of the stars in the pan, cover, and cook on each side for 2–3 minutes, or until well browned. Let cool to room temperature. Repeat with remaining bread slices.

To serve, spread cream filling over 8 stars using 1/4 cup for each; place on individual serving plates. Sprinkle 1/2 cup blueberries and 1/2 cup strawberries over cream filling. Set remaining stars over top and dust with powdered sugar, if desired. Spoon syrup, if using, generously over stacks and garnish with a dollop of cream filling.

fondue party

MAKES 6 TO 8 SERVINGS

You'll forget about boring cubes of angel food cake once you start dipping warm cubes of French toast into sweet syrups, delectable cookie crumbs, and fresh fruit.

- 2 cups milk
- ½ cup flour
- 6 large eggs
- 1 tablespoon vanilla
- 1 teaspoon salt
- 1 loaf day-old French bread
- Butter
- Diced fresh fruits, chopped nuts, and shredded coconut
- Crumbled sugar cookies or other favorite cookies
- 1 or 2 specialty syrups (pages 116–125)

In a pie plate or other shallow pan, whisk together the milk and flour; whisk in eggs, vanilla, and salt.

Cut bread into 2-inch cubes, leaving crust on one side of each chunk. Soak bread chunks in egg mixture for 10–20 seconds on each side, or until just soaked through.

Melt a little butter in a small frying pan over medium-high heat. Working in small batches, add soaked bread to the pan and cook each side for 1–2 minutes, or until lightly browned. Place on a baking tray in a warm oven to keep until ready to serve.

Place fruits, nuts, coconut, and cookie crumbs on individual serving plates or in bowls. Pour syrup into a fondue pot and place warm bread cubes in a large bowl or on a serving platter. Pierce bread cubes with toothpicks or skewers, crust side first; dip in syrup and favorite topping.

casseroles and bakes

christmas morning casserole MAKES 6 TO 8 SERVINGS

Begin a delicious new holiday tradition with eggnog French toast. Don't forget to invite Santa!

2 1/2 cups eggnog

3 large eggs

1 teaspoon nutmeg

1 teaspoon cinnamon

1/2 teaspoon salt

1 large loaf French bread

Cranapple Compote (page 119)

In a bowl, whisk together the eggnog, eggs, nutmeg, cinnamon, and salt. Pour half of the eggnog mixture into a 9 x 13-inch baking pan. Cut ends off bread and discard. Cut bread into 8 slices, about 1 1/2 inches thick, and arrange in the pan. Pour remaining eggnog mixture evenly over the bread, cover, and refrigerate overnight. Remove from refrigerator and turn bread slices over; bring to room temperature, about 30 minutes.

Preheat oven to 425 degrees.

Bake, uncovered, for 20 minutes. Carefully turn bread slices and bake 10–15 minutes more, or until puffed and browned. Serve with Cranapple Compote.

french twist casserole

MAKES 4 TO 6 SERVINGS

The elegantly spiraled croissants combined with Maple Cream Syrup make this a sinfully rich dining experience.

- **1 cup Maple Cream Syrup (page 116), divided**
- **6 large (6-inch) day-old croissants**
- **3 large eggs**
- **1 cup milk**
- **½ teaspoon salt**
- **1 teaspoon vanilla**

Spray a round 2 ½-quart baking dish generously with nonstick cooking spray. Pour ⅓ cup of syrup into the bottom of the pan. Cut croissants in half through the wide middle so that each piece has a curved end. Overlap croissants around the side of the pan like a fan, with the pointed ends facing down in the center.

In a small bowl, whisk together the eggs, milk, salt, and vanilla; pour over croissants. Cover and refrigerate a few hours or overnight. Remove from refrigerator and bring to room temperature, about 30 minutes. Pour remaining ⅔ cup of syrup evenly over top.

Preheat oven to 350 degrees.

Bake, uncovered, for 45–50 minutes, or until browned and liquid is completely absorbed.

triple strawberries and cream MAKES 6 SERVINGS

This sweet classic combination will become the dish everyone begs you to make.

12 (1-inch-thick) slices day-old French bread, crusts removed

6 ounces light cream cheese, softened

½ cup low-sugar strawberry jam

4 large eggs

2 cups milk

2 tablespoons sugar

1 teaspoon salt

2 cups sliced fresh strawberries

1 cup strawberry syrup

Whipped cream

Spray a 9 x 13-inch baking pan with nonstick cooking spray.

Spread 1 side of 6 bread slices with 1 tablespoon cream cheese. Equally divide and spread jam on 1 side of remaining bread slices. Lightly press cream cheese and jam slices together to seal. Arrange sandwiches in the pan.

In a bowl, whisk together the eggs, milk, sugar, and salt. Pour half of the egg mixture over the sandwiches. Cover and refrigerate at least 2 hours or overnight. Remove from refrigerator and carefully turn sandwiches over; pour remaining egg mixture over top. Bring to room temperature, about 30 minutes.

Preheat oven to 350 degrees.

Bake, uncovered, for 35–40 minutes, or until golden brown. Cut into squares and serve with strawberries, syrup, and a dollop of whipped cream on top.

peach cobbler MAKES 6 TO 8 SERVINGS

All the taste of classic peach cobbler in a French toast dish.

6 large eggs

1 cup milk

1/2 cup sweetened condensed milk

8 cups (1-inch cubes) day-old French bread

6 cups fresh or frozen (thawed) peach chunks

3 tablespoons cornstarch

1/2 cup sugar

2 tablespoons fresh-squeezed lemon juice

1 cup flour

1 teaspoon cinnamon

1/3 cup brown sugar

6 tablespoons cold butter, cut into small pieces

Whipped cream or ice cream, optional

Preheat oven to 400 degrees.

In a large bowl, whisk together the eggs, milk, and condensed milk. Add bread cubes, tossing until evenly coated; set aside. Toss with a spoon occasionally to make sure liquid is evenly absorbed.

In a separate bowl, toss peaches with cornstarch, sugar, and lemon juice. Place in a 4-quart baking dish that has been sprayed with nonstick cooking spray. Spread soaked bread cubes evenly over top.

In another bowl, whisk together the flour, cinnamon, and brown sugar. Cut in the butter with a pastry cutter or fork until the mixture resembles small peas; scatter evenly over top of casserole.

Bake, uncovered, for 30–40 minutes, or until cooked through and bubbly around the edges. Serve topped with whipped cream or ice cream, if desired.

pecan praline

MAKES 6 TO 8 SERVINGS

The soothing spices and subtle nuttiness of this dish will fill your tummy with goodness.

1 loaf day-old French bread
6 large eggs
1/4 teaspoon nutmeg
1/2 teaspoon cinnamon
1/2 teaspoon salt
1 tablespoon vanilla
3 cups milk
1/4 cup butter, softened
2 tablespoons corn syrup
1 cup light brown sugar
1 cup chopped pecans

Spray a 9 x 13-inch baking pan with nonstick cooking spray.

Slice bread into 8 (1 1/2-inch-thick) slices; arrange in pan. In a bowl, whisk together the eggs, spices, salt, vanilla, and milk. Pour egg mixture evenly over bread slices, cover, and refrigerate overnight. Remove from refrigerator and turn bread slices over in the pan; bring to room temperature, about 30 minutes.

Preheat oven to 350 degrees.

In a bowl, combine the butter, syrup, sugar, and pecans. Sprinkle mixture over bread slices. Bake, uncovered, for 50 minutes. Remove from oven and let stand 10 minutes before serving.

streusel topped MAKES 6 TO 8 SERVINGS

The aroma of this coffee cake-style breakfast casserole baking will wake even the soundest of sleepers.

4 eggs

2 cups milk

1 teaspoon cinnamon

½ teaspoon salt

4 tablespoons vanilla

⅓ cup sugar

1 large loaf day-old French bread

streusel topping

⅓ cup brown sugar

¼ cup butter

1 tablespoon flour

⅓ cup quick oats

½ teaspoon cinnamon

¼ cup chopped pecans

Spray a 9 x 13-inch baking pan with nonstick cooking spray.

In a bowl, whisk together the eggs, milk, cinnamon, salt, vanilla, and sugar. Pour half of the mixture into the pan. Cut bread into 1 ½-inch-thick slices and lay in the pan, filling completely. Pour remaining egg mixture over top, cover, and refrigerate overnight. Remove from refrigerator and bring to room temperature, about 30 minutes.

Preheat oven to 450 degrees.

Bake, uncovered, for 15 minutes. Meanwhile, combine the topping ingredients together in a small bowl and sprinkle evenly over casserole; bake for 10 more minutes.

pineapple upside down bake

MAKES 6 SERVINGS

French toast is the perfect way to pay homage to this pineapple classic.

- 1/4 cup butter
- 1/2 cup brown sugar
- 2 tablespoons corn syrup
- 1 (20-ounce) can pineapple rings, drained, 1/4 cup juice reserved
- 6 maraschino cherries
- 6 slices day-old Texas-style toast, or thickly sliced, firm white bread
- 3 large eggs
- 1 cup milk
- 1/2 teaspoon salt
- 1/2 teaspoon cinnamon
- 1 teaspoon vanilla

Spray a 9 x 13-inch baking pan with nonstick cooking spray.

In a small frying pan, heat the butter, sugar, and syrup until sugar is dissolved, stirring occasionally. Pour mixture into pan and spread evenly. Place 6 pineapple rings in pan, evenly spaced apart so each ring will be in the center of a bread slice. Place a cherry in the center of each ring. Arrange bread slices over pineapple rings, pressing bread slightly with a spatula into the rings.

In a bowl, whisk together eggs, milk, salt, cinnamon, and vanilla; pour evenly over bread, saturating each slice. Cover and refrigerate at least 2 hours or overnight. Remove from refrigerator and bring to room temperature, about 30 minutes.

Preheat oven to 375 degrees.

Bake, uncovered, for 40–45 minutes, or until puffed and lightly browned. Let cool for about 10 minutes before inverting onto a serving platter so the pineapple rings are on top.

blueberries and cream soufflé MAKES 6 TO 8 SERVINGS

This delicious berry casserole could become a true blue favorite.

- 2 (8-ounce) packages Neufchâtel or light cream cheese, divided
- 10 cups (1-inch cubes) day-old French bread
- 1 tablespoon lemon zest
- 2 cups fresh or frozen blueberries
- 8 large eggs, at room temperature
- 2 1/2 cups milk, at room temperature, divided
- 1/2 cup pure maple syrup
- Blueberry Syrup (page 118)
- Powdered sugar, optional

Spray a 3 1/2- to 4-quart casserole dish generously with nonstick cooking spray. Cut one of the cream cheese packages into small cubes. Place in a large bowl along with the bread, zest, and blueberries, tossing to combine; place in casserole dish. Soften the remaining cream cheese in the microwave for 60 seconds.

In a separate bowl, whisk together the softened cream cheese, eggs, 2 cups milk, and maple syrup; pour evenly over bread mixture. Cover and refrigerate 2 hours or overnight. Remove from refrigerator and bring to room temperature, about 30 minutes. Pour remaining 1/2 cup milk over top.

Preheat oven to 350 degrees.

Cover and bake for 20 minutes; uncover and bake for 30 minutes more, or until lightly browned and set in the center. Serve with Blueberry Syrup and a sprinkling of powdered sugar, if desired.

VARIATION: *Once mixture is ready to bake, it can be divided into individual ramekins and baked for 30–35 minutes, or until lightly browned and set in the center.*

sticky buns MAKES 6 TO 8 SERVINGS

Try this gooey cinnamon French toast to satisfy your craving for cinnamon rolls–an easy crowd pleaser.

½ cup butter

1 cup brown sugar

3 tablespoons corn syrup

½ cup roughly chopped pecans

8 (1-inch-thick) slices day-old French bread

6 large eggs

1½ cups milk

1 teaspoon vanilla

1 teaspoon cinnamon

½ teaspoon salt

Spray a 9 x 13-inch baking pan with nonstick cooking spray.

In a saucepan over medium-high heat, melt butter and sugar until sugar is dissolved, stirring constantly; add syrup and cook until thickened, 2–3 minutes. Pour mixture into pan and sprinkle nuts over top. Place bread slices over nuts, forming a single layer.

In a bowl, whisk together the eggs, milk, vanilla, cinnamon, and salt; pour over bread slices, saturating evenly. Cover and refrigerate 2 hours or overnight. Remove from refrigerator and bring to room temperature, about 30 minutes.

Preheat oven to 350 degrees.

Bake, uncovered, for 45–50 minutes, or until lightly browned. Let stand 10 minutes before inverting onto a serving plate.

rise 'n' shine breakfast soufflé

MAKES 4 TO 6 SERVINGS

This savory breakfast dish is the perfect combination of eggs, bacon, and cheese.

- 1 loaf day-old French bread, cubed (about 12 cups)
- 8 ounces sharp cheddar cheese, grated
- 1/2 cup chopped fresh flat-leaf parsley
- 8 large eggs
- 4 cups milk
- 1 teaspoon dry mustard
- 1 teaspoon seasoned salt
- 1/2 teaspoon white pepper
- 1/2 cup diced tomatoes
- 1/2 cup cooked and crumbled bacon

Generously spray a 4-quart baking dish with nonstick cooking spray. Toss bread cubes with half of the cheese and place in baking dish. Sprinkle remaining cheese and parsley over top.

In a bowl, whisk together the eggs, milk, and spices. Pour egg mixture over bread and cheese. Sprinkle tomatoes and bacon on top, cover, and refrigerate overnight. Remove from refrigerator and bring to room temperature, about 30 minutes.

Preheat oven to 375 degrees.

Bake, uncovered, for 45–50 minutes, or until puffed and lightly golden brown on top.

shrimp croissant casserole MAKES 4 SERVINGS

An easy yet elegant casserole filled with the savory tastes of shrimp, cheese, and onion.

- 4 large day-old croissants, torn into 1-inch pieces
- 8 ounces grated Monterey Jack or Havarti cheese
- 8 ounces cooked tiny cocktail shrimp
- 3 green onions, thinly sliced
- 4 large eggs
- 1 ½ cups milk
- ½ teaspoon salt
- ½ teaspoon white pepper

Spray an 8 x 11-inch baking pan with nonstick cooking spray, spreading half of the croissant pieces in the bottom. Sprinkle half of the cheese evenly over the top followed by the shrimp and onions. Spread remaining croissant pieces over shrimp and sprinkle with remaining cheese.

In a bowl, whisk together the eggs, milk, salt, and pepper; pour evenly over mixture in pan. Cover and refrigerate for several hours or overnight. Remove from refrigerator and bring to room temperature, about 30 minutes.

Preheat oven to 350 degrees.

Bake, uncovered, for 40–45 minutes, or until firm. Let stand for 10 minutes before serving.

hazelnut breakfast ring

MAKES 8 TO 10 SERVINGS

This caramelized and nutty breakfast delight is incredibly easy to prepare, and looks gorgeous on a serving platter prominently set in the center of the table.

4 large eggs

1 (16-ounce) bottle liquid hazelnut coffee creamer

½ cup milk

½ teaspoon nutmeg

12 cups (1-inch cubes) day-old French bread

1 cup roughly chopped hazelnuts

1 cup dark brown sugar

1 teaspoon cinnamon

Syrup, of choice, optional

Preheat oven to 375 degrees. Generously spray a 2 ½-quart bundt pan with nonstick cooking spray.

In a bowl, whisk together the eggs, creamer, milk, and nutmeg. Toss bread cubes in egg mixture and let stand about 3 minutes, tossing a few times to make sure liquid is absorbed evenly.

In a small bowl, mix together the nuts, brown sugar, and cinnamon. Sprinkle about ½ of the nut mixture in the bottom of the pan. Spread ½ cup bread cubes in pan, pressing with a large spoon to remove air pockets. Sprinkle remaining nut mixture over top. Spread remaining bread cubes over nut mixture, pressing again to remove air pockets.

Bake, uncovered, for 35–40 minutes, or until firm. Let stand for about 10 minutes before inverting onto a serving platter. To serve, cut into slices and drizzle with syrup, if desired.

nutty cinnamon raisin breakfast MAKES 4 TO 6 SERVINGS

This dish has just the right medley of crunchy, creamy, and fruity—a little something to please everyone.

- 1 (16-ounce) loaf day-old cinnamon raisin bread
- 1/2 cup roughly chopped pecans
- 1 (20-ounce) can crushed pineapple, with juice
- 1/4 cup butter, melted
- 4 large eggs
- 1/2 cup sugar
- 1/2 cup milk
- 1/2 teaspoon salt
- Powdered sugar, optional
- Syrup, of choice, optional

Preheat oven to 375 degrees. Spray an 8 x 11-inch baking pan with nonstick cooking spray.

Cut the bread into 1-inch pieces, place in a bowl with the pecans, pineapple and juice, and toss to coat; spread mixture in the pan.

In a bowl, whisk together the butter, eggs, sugar, milk, and salt. Pour over bread mixture, making sure the bread is saturated; let stand 20 minutes. Bake, uncovered, for 35–40 minutes, or until firm and lightly browned.

To serve, cut into squares and sprinkle with powdered sugar or a drizzle of syrup, if desired.

crab strata supreme

MAKES 6 TO 8 SERVINGS

You'll enjoy delicious layers of crab, onion, mushrooms, cheese, and more in this flavorful casserole.

2 tablespoons butter

1 red bell pepper, diced

3 green onions, thinly sliced

8 ounces diced mushrooms

2 cups diced celery

10 cups (1-inch cubes) day-old French bread

8 ounces crabmeat, diced

2 cups grated Swiss or Havarti cheese

8 large eggs

2 cups milk

1 cup sour cream

¼ cup dry white wine or white grape juice

1 teaspoon dry mustard

½ teaspoon each salt and white pepper

½ cup grated Parmesan cheese

Spray a 3 ½- to 4-quart casserole dish with nonstick cooking spray.

In a frying pan over medium-high heat, sauté butter, bell pepper, onions, mushrooms, and celery until onion is translucent, about 3 minutes. Toss sautéed mixture in a large bowl with the bread cubes and spread in bottom of casserole dish. Sprinkle crab and Swiss cheese evenly over top.

In a bowl, whisk together remaining ingredients except Parmesan cheese; pour over crab. Cover and refrigerate several hours or overnight. Remove from refrigerator and bring to room temperature, about 30 minutes.

Preheat oven to 350 degrees.

Bake, covered, for 30 minutes. Sprinkle Parmesan cheese over top and bake, uncovered, for 15 more minutes. Let stand for 10 minutes before serving.

peach melba casserole

MAKES 4 TO 6 SERVINGS

A decadent breakfast treat and a great new twist on the traditional peach and raspberry dessert.

4 large eggs, divided

2 cups half-and-half

1/2 cup sugar

1 teaspoon vanilla

1/2 teaspoon salt

2 to 3 pinches nutmeg

12 to 14 slices day-old firm white bread, crusts removed

8 ounces cream cheese, softened

3 tablespoons peach jam

2 large ripe peaches, peeled and thinly sliced

Raspberry Syrup (page 118)

In a bowl, whisk together 3 eggs, half-and-half, sugar, vanilla, salt, and nutmeg. Pour 1/2 of the egg mixture into a 9 x 13-inch baking pan. Arrange 1/2 of the bread slices over the egg mixture, completely covering the bottom.

In a bowl, mix together the cream cheese, 1 egg, and jam; spread over bread slices. Arrange peach slices on top in a single layer. Place remaining bread slices over peaches, completely covering surface. Pour remaining egg mixture evenly over top. Cover and refrigerate 2 hours or overnight. Remove from refrigerator and bring to room temperature, about 30 minutes.

Preheat oven to 350 degrees.

Bake, uncovered, for 30–40 minutes, or until golden brown on top. Serve hot with Raspberry Syrup.

ciabatta, gruyère, and sausage bake

MAKES 6 TO 8 SERVINGS

The crusty bread, cheese, and sausage make this French toast variation a delightful combination of flavors and textures.

- **8 ounces large turkey or chicken sausages, casings removed**
- **1 (16-ounce) loaf day-old ciabatta or panini**
- **½ cup thinly sliced green onions**
- **½ cup chopped fresh flat-leaf parsley**
- **8 ounces grated Gruyère cheese**
- **2 ½ cups milk**
- **6 large eggs**
- **½ teaspoon salt**

Spray a 9 x 13-inch baking pan with nonstick cooking spray.

Crumble sausages into a preheated frying pan. Cook over high heat until lightly browned; remove from heat. Cut bread into 1-inch cubes and toss with cooked sausage, onions, parsley, and cheese in a large bowl. Spread bread mixture in pan.

In a bowl, whisk together the milk, eggs, and salt; pour over bread mixture, saturating bread evenly. Cover and refrigerate 2 hours or overnight. Remove from refrigerator and bring to room temperature, about 30 minutes.

Preheat oven to 350 degrees.

Bake, uncovered, for 45–50 minutes, or until cooked through and lightly browned on top.

caramelized pear casserole MAKES 6 TO 8 SERVINGS

This breakfast delight will wake up the household with its tempting pear and cinnamon combination.

4 tablespoons butter

2 large Bosc pears, peeled, cored, and cut in 1/4-inch-thick slices

1 cup light brown sugar

4 tablespoons light corn syrup

1 loaf challah or French bread, cut in 1-inch-thick slices

6 eggs

2 cups milk

1 teaspoon cinnamon

1/4 teaspoon nutmeg

1 teaspoon vanilla

1/2 teaspoon salt

Over high heat, melt butter in a medium frying pan and sauté pears for 2–3 minutes, or until lightly browned, stirring constantly to release moisture from pears. Remove pears and spread evenly in the bottom of a 9 x 13-inch pan.

Add sugar and syrup to the frying pan and heat to a simmer. Cook 1–2 minutes, or until sugar is dissolved. Pour sugar mixture over pears and lay bread slices over top, completely filling pan.

In a bowl, whisk together remaining ingredients and pour over bread, saturating evenly. Cover and refrigerate 2 hours or overnight. Remove from refrigerator and bring to room temperature, about 30 minutes.

Preheat oven to 350 degrees.

Bake, uncovered, for 45–50 minutes, or until cooked through and lightly browned on top.

savory entrées

french toast chili stacks MAKES 4 SERVINGS

With the smoky kick of chipotle, this recipe will soon become a favorite go-to meal.

1 large egg

1 cup milk

1/4 cup flour

1/2 teaspoon salt

2 teaspoons chipotle chile powder

4 (7-inch diameter) day-old flatbreads or soft pita bread rounds

Butter

4 cups chili, any kind, heated

2 cups grated cheddar cheese, divided

Diced lettuce, tomato, and onion

In a pie plate or other shallow pan, whisk together the egg, milk, flour, salt, and chile powder. Soak flatbreads 1 at a time in egg mixture for 3–5 minutes on each side, or until soaked through and softened. (The softer the flatbread or pitas, the less soaking time is needed.)

Melt a little butter in an 8-inch frying pan over medium-high heat. Cook soaked flatbread in covered pan 1 at a time for 2–3 minutes on each side, or until well browned. Place 1 cooked flatbread on a microwave-safe plate, spread 1 cup chili over top and sprinkle with 1/2 cup cheese; microwave for 30–60 seconds, or until bubbly around edges and cheese has melted. Top with lettuce, tomato, and onion, as desired.

cheesy chile strata MAKES 4 TO 6 SERVINGS

The blend of chiles and cheese will make this dish a new mealtime favorite.

3 Anaheim chiles

1 jalapeño

8 cups (1-inch cubes) day-old French bread

8 ounces grated sharp cheddar cheese

4 ounces grated sharp white cheddar or Monterey Jack cheese

½ cup thinly sliced green onion

½ cup chopped fresh cilantro

6 large eggs, beaten

2 cups milk

1 tablespoon ground cumin

1 teaspoon chipotle chile powder

1 teaspoon salt

Salsa, of choice

Preheat oven to 375 degrees. Prepare a 4-quart casserole with nonstick cooking spray.

Slice chiles and jalapeño in half lengthwise and remove seeds and ribs. Grill or broil for 3–5 minutes, or until skins are blackened. Place in a ziplock bag and allow to sweat for 5 minutes. Remove skins and dice.

In a large bowl, toss together the bread cubes, chiles, cheeses, onion, and cilantro; place in casserole dish. In a separate bowl, whisk together the eggs, milk, cumin, chile powder, and salt. Pour over bread mixture, making sure the bread is completely saturated. Bake, uncovered, for 35–40 minutes, or until lightly browned and almost set in the center. Serve with salsa on top, or on the side.

tomato basil monte cristos MAKES 4 SANDWICHES

This fresh take on the classic sandwich will turn lunch into a little taste of France.

- 1/2 cup flour
- 1 1/2 cups seasoned toasted breadcrumbs
- 4 large eggs
- 1/2 cup milk
- 4 (1/4-inch-thick) slices mozzarella cheese
- 8 slices day-old firm white bread
- 1 bunch fresh basil, chopped
- 1 large vine-ripened tomato, thinly sliced

Spread flour and breadcrumbs on separate plates. In a pie plate or other shallow pan, whisk together the eggs and milk. Place a slice of cheese on 4 of the bread slices. Sprinkle a little basil over the cheese and add some tomato slices; top with remaining bread.

Heat a small frying pan that has been sprayed with nonstick cooking spray over medium heat. Coat the outsides of each sandwich by first dipping in the flour, then the egg mixture, and finally the breadcrumbs. Place 1 of the sandwiches in the pan, cover, and cook on each side for about 2 minutes, or until golden brown. Repeat with remaining sandwiches.

pepper jelly monte cristos MAKES 4 SANDWICHES

Pepper Jack cheese helps add a little kick to this perfectly flavored sandwich.

1/2 cup flour

1 1/2 cups seasoned toasted breadcrumbs

4 large eggs

1/2 cup milk

4 tablespoons jalapeño jelly

8 slices day-old firm white bread

8 tablespoons thinly sliced green onion

4 (1/4-inch-thick) slices pepper Jack cheese

4 slices deli ham

4 slices deli smoked turkey

Spread out the flour and breadcrumbs on separate plates. In a pie plate or other shallow pan, whisk together the eggs and milk.

Spread 1 tablespoon jelly on each of 4 bread slices. Sprinkle 1 tablespoon green onion over jelly, followed by 1 cheese slice, 1 ham slice, and 1 turkey slice; top with remaining bread slices.

Heat a small frying pan that has been sprayed with nonstick cooking spray over medium heat. Coat the outsides of each sandwich by first dipping in the flour, then the egg mixture, and finally the breadcrumbs. Place 1 of the sandwiches in the pan, cover, and cook on each side for about 2 minutes, or until golden brown. Repeat with remaining sandwiches.

ham, swiss, and caramelized onions

MAKES 4 SANDWICHES

Ham and Swiss sandwiches topped with caramelized onions for the win!

- ½ cup flour
- 1½ cups seasoned toasted breadcrumbs
- 4 large eggs
- ½ cup milk
- 2 tablespoons butter
- 1 large Vidalia or yellow onion, julienned
- ¼ teaspoon nutmeg, optional
- 8 slices baby Swiss or Havarti cheese
- 8 slices day-old firm white bread
- 4 slices deli ham

Spread out the flour and breadcrumbs on separate plates. In a pie plate or other shallow pan, whisk together the eggs and milk. Melt the butter in a medium frying pan over medium-high heat, and sauté onion until caramelized and lightly browned; stir in nutmeg, if using. Place 1 cheese slice on 4 of the bread slices. Spread ½ cup onion mixture over the cheese. Layer 1 ham slice over onions followed by another cheese slice; top with remaining bread slices.

Heat a small frying pan that has been sprayed with nonstick cooking spray over medium heat. Coat both sides of each sandwich by first dipping in the flour, then the egg mixture, and finally the breadcrumbs. Place 1 of the sandwiches in the pan, cover, and cook on each side for about 2 minutes, or until golden brown and cheese has started to melt. Repeat with remaining sandwiches.

french onion baked monte cristos

MAKES 4 SANDWICHES

This classic sandwich with French onion taste baked right into the bread is one your family will ask for again and again.

- 4 large eggs
- 1 cup milk
- 1 envelope dry French onion soup mix
- 8 slices day-old firm white bread
- 8 slices Swiss cheese
- 4 slices deli ham
- 4 slices deli turkey
- 1/2 cup sour cream
- 2 tablespoons Dijon mustard

Preheat oven to 425 degrees. Prepare a 9 x 13-inch baking pan with nonstick cooking spray.

In a pie plate or other shallow pan, whisk together the eggs, milk, and soup mix. Soak 1 side of 4 bread slices in egg mixture for about 30 seconds. Place soaked side down in baking pan. Layer 1 cheese slice, 1 ham slice, 1 turkey slice, and 1 more cheese slice over top of each bread slice in pan. Soak 1 side of remaining bread slices in egg mixture for 30 seconds. Place dry side down on top of cheese.

Bake, uncovered, for 5 minutes. Remove from oven and carefully turn each sandwich over. Return to oven and bake 5 minutes more. Turn oven to broil for 1 minute; turn off oven and let sandwiches sit a few minutes more before removing.

In a small bowl, mix together the sour cream and mustard. Serve sandwiches hot with sour cream mixture drizzled over top or served on the side.

tuscan supper strata

MAKES 4 TO 6 SERVINGS

A taste of Italy is only minutes away with this combination of prosciutto, mozzarella, Parmesan, basil, and tomato. Mangia!

- 8 cups (1-inch cubes) day-old French bread
- 8 ounces fresh mozzarella, cut into tiny cubes
- 8 ounces thinly sliced prosciutto, chopped
- 3 large ripe tomatoes, diced
- 5 large eggs
- 1 1/2 cups milk
- 1/2 cup sour cream
- 1 teaspoon Italian seasoning
- 1 teaspoon dried basil
- 1/2 teaspoon salt
- 1/2 teaspoon garlic powder
- 1/2 cup freshly grated Parmesan cheese

Prepare a 9 x 13-inch baking pan with nonstick cooking spray.

Toss bread cubes, cheese, prosciutto, and tomatoes together in a large bowl; spread bread mixture in pan.

In a separate bowl, whisk together the eggs, milk,sour cream, seasoning, basil, salt, and garlic powder. Pour evenly over bread mixture, thoroughly saturating. Cover and refrigerate 2 hours or overnight. Remove from refrigerator and bring to room temperature, about 30 minutes.

Preheat oven to 350 degrees.

Bake, uncovered, for 40–45 minutes, or until firm and lightly browned. Sprinkle with Parmesan cheese.

savory cheddar crusted french toast MAKES 8 TOASTS

The cheese in this recipe magically coats the bread and forms a crunchy golden brown crust.

2 large eggs

1 cup milk

1/2 cup sour cream

1/2 teaspoon salt

3 cups finely grated sharp cheddar cheese

1/2 cup freshly grated Parmesan cheese

1 tablespoon flour

1 teaspoon garlic powder

1 tablespoon Italian seasoning

8 (1-inch-thick) slices day-old French bread

In a pie plate or other shallow pan, whisk together the eggs, milk, sour cream, and salt until smooth. In a bowl, toss together the cheeses, flour, garlic powder, and seasoning. Soak bread slices in egg mixture for about 60 seconds on each side.

Heat a small frying pan sprayed with nonstick cooking spray over medium-high heat. Place 1 soaked bread slice in pan and cook, uncovered, for about 2 minutes, or until lightly browned; flip, and spread 2 tablespoons cheese mixture evenly over cooked side. After about 2 minutes, flip bread over again and spread 2 table-spoons of cheese mixture evenly on side now facing up. After about 2 minutes, flip bread over. Cook another 1–2 minutes, or until the cheese on the other side is crisp and browned. Repeat with remaining bread slices.

tangy chipotle cornbread MAKES 8 SERVINGS

Try this fun, fast, and flavorful twist on tamale pie.

$^3/_4$ cup cornmeal

$^1/_4$ cup flour

2 teaspoons chipotle chile powder

3 large eggs

1 cup milk

$^1/_2$ teaspoon salt

8 ($^1/_2$-inch-thick) slices sturdy day-old cornbread

Canola oil

1 (15-ounce) can black beans, drained and rinsed

1 (12-ounce) can red enchilada sauce

6 ounces crumbled queso fresco

1 tomato, diced

1 bunch fresh cilantro, chopped

Mix together the cornmeal, flour, and chile powder on a large plate. In a pie plate or other shallow pan, whisk together the eggs, milk, and salt. Dip both sides of cornbread slices first in egg mixture and then in the cornmeal mixture.

Heat a small frying pan with a little oil over medium heat. Cook battered cornbread slices on each side for 2–3 minutes, or until golden brown.

Place beans and enchilada sauce in a blender and blend until smooth. Place in a microwave-safe bowl and heat in microwave for about 90 seconds. To serve, top cornbread slices with bean sauce, cheese, tomato, and cilantro.

savory eggs in a basket MAKES 6 SERVINGS

This recipe is easily whipped up in about 20 minutes, for a savory meal that can be enjoyed at breakfast, lunch, or even dinner.

8 large eggs, divided

1/2 cup milk

1/2 teaspoon garlic powder

1/2 teaspoon seasoned salt

6 slices day-old firm white bread, crusts removed

1 cup grated cheddar cheese

Preheat oven to 400 degrees. Spray 6 (1-cup) jumbo muffin cups or ramekins generously with nonstick cooking spray.

In a pie plate or other shallow pan, whisk together 2 eggs, milk, garlic powder, and salt. Dip bread slices into egg mixture for 10 seconds on each side, and then press each slice lightly into a muffin cup, forming a basket (corners of bread slices will be sticking out of muffin cups). Crack 1 egg into each of the baskets and sprinkle a little cheese over top. Bake for 15 minutes for a slightly runny center, or bake longer for a more set egg yolk, as desired.

seafood newberg stacks MAKES 6 SERVINGS

You'll be hooked on the flavor-packed combination of lobster bisque and shrimp, and how quick and easy this fresh take on an American classic dish comes together.

3 green onions, thinly sliced

1/2 green bell pepper, diced

1 tablespoon butter

1 (14-ounce) can condensed lobster or shrimp bisque

1/2 pound cooked and peeled shrimp, diced

1/2 pound cooked scallops, diced

1/2 pound cooked regular or imitation crab, chopped

1 cup half-and-half

3 large eggs

1/2 teaspoon salt

6 day-old English muffins, split

In a large frying pan, sauté onions and bell pepper in butter over medium heat until limp but not browned; stir in bisque. Add the shrimp, scallops, and crab to soup mixture, and cook until hot and bubbly around edges; reduce heat and cover to keep warm.

In a pie plate or other shallow pan, whisk together the half-and-half, eggs, and salt. Dip muffin halves in egg mixture for a few seconds on each side, gently shaking off any excess. Heat a small frying pan sprayed with nonstick cooking spray over medium heat. Add 1 soaked muffin half to the pan, cover, and cook on each side for about 3 minutes. Repeat with remaining halves.

To serve, top 1 muffin half with 1/3 cup seafood mixture, second half of the muffin, and another 1/3 cup seafood.

french toast pizzas

MAKES 6 SERVINGS

These easy and flavorful individual pizzas are the perfect size to satisfy that late-night craving.

1 cup milk

1/4 cup flour

3 large eggs

1/2 teaspoon salt

Butter

6 (8-inch diameter) day-old pita rounds or flatbreads

3 cups pizza sauce

1 1/2 cups grated mozzarella cheese

Pizza toppings, of choice, such as pepperoni, olives, green peppers, or onions

1/2 cup grated Parmesan cheese

Preheat oven to 400 degrees. Prepare a wire baking rack with nonstick cooking spray and set on a baking sheet.

In a pie plate or other shallow pan, whisk together the milk and flour; whisk in eggs and salt. Soak each pita for 10–20 seconds on each side, or until just soaked through. Melt a little butter in a medium frying pan over medium-high heat. Add 1 soaked pita to the pan, cover, and cook on each side for 1–2 minutes, or until lightly browned. Repeat with remaining pitas.

Place pitas on wire rack and bake for 10 minutes. Remove from oven and spread 1/2 cup pizza sauce over each pita; sprinkle 1/4 cup mozzarella cheese and desired toppings over top. Turn oven to broil and place baking sheet on top rack. Broil pizzas until cheese melts and starts to bubble, watching closely so as not to burn. Sprinkle with Parmesan before serving.

30-minute skillet strata MAKES 4 TO 6 SERVINGS

This quick version of a classic strata is a lot less fussy, but doesn't skimp on flavor.

6 large eggs

1 1/2 cups milk

1 cup grated sharp cheddar cheese

2 tablespoons dried parsley

1 teaspoon seasoned salt

1/4 cup butter

1 medium yellow onion, diced

1/2 cup cooked diced meat*, of choice

4 cups day-old firm white bread cubes

Preheat oven to 425 degrees.

In a large bowl, whisk together the eggs, milk, cheese, parsley, and salt. Melt butter in a 10-inch ovenproof frying pan and cook onion over medium-high heat until translucent, about 3 minutes. Stir in meat and bread cubes and cook another 3–5 minutes, or until bread is coated and lightly toasted. Turn off heat and stir in egg mixture, mixing just until all the bread cubes are soaked.

Place pan in oven and bake for 16–18 minutes, or until puffed and golden brown and center is set.

*TRY *sausage, bacon, ham, smoked salmon, or tiny cocktail shrimp.*

kentucky hot browns

MAKES 8 SERVINGS

A Southern favorite, this open-faced sandwich comes together in a snap.

3 large eggs

3 cups milk, divided

2 teaspoons salt, divided

8 slices day-old firm white bread

8 (1/4-inch-thick) slices cooked turkey

3 tablespoons butter

2 tablespoons flour

4 ounces grated extra sharp white cheddar cheese

1/2 cup grated Parmesan cheese

1/4 teaspoon nutmeg

1 teaspoon white pepper

4 large ripe tomatoes, sliced 1/4-inch thick

8 slices bacon, cooked and crumbled

Prepare a baking sheet with nonstick cooking spray.

In a pie plate or other shallow pan, mix together eggs, 1/2 cup milk, and 1 teaspoon salt. Soak bread slices in egg mixture for 30 seconds on each side. Heat a small frying pan sprayed with nonstick cooking spray over medium-high heat. Add 1 soaked bread slice to the pan, cover, and cook on each side for 2–3 minutes, or until lightly browned. Repeat with remaining bread. Place cooked bread slices on baking sheet and top each with 1 slice of turkey.

Preheat oven to broil.

In a small saucepan, melt butter over medium-high heat. Add flour and cook 1 minute, stirring constantly. Whisk in remaining milk and simmer until thickened, 3–4 minutes. Add cheeses, 1 teaspoon salt, nutmeg, and pepper; stir until cheese has melted and remove from heat. Ladle sauce over turkey and bread slices. Place in oven and broil 3–5 minutes, or until golden brown. Layer tomato slices over top and sprinkle with bacon.

smoked salmon bagels MAKES 6 SERVINGS

This New York deli-style French toast makes a great brunch for a lazy day.

3 large eggs

1 cup milk

½ teaspoon salt

3 savory day-old bagels

Butter

½ cup whipped cream cheese

3 tablespoons minced fresh dill

6 ounces sliced smoked Nova Scotia-style salmon

6 tablespoons minced fresh flat-leaf parsley

Capers, optional

In a pie plate or other shallow pan, whisk together the eggs, milk, and salt. Cut bagels in half and soak each half in egg mixture for about 1 minute on each side.

Melt a little butter in a small frying pan over medium-high heat. Add 1 soaked bagel half to the pan, cover, and cook on each side for 2–3 minutes, or until lightly browned. Repeat with remaining bagels.

Place on individual plates and cool to room temperature. When ready to serve, spread a thick layer of cream cheese on cut side of each bagel. Sprinkle ½ tablespoon dill over cream cheese and top with 1–2 slices of salmon, cutting to fit so the salmon hangs slightly over sides of bagel. Sprinkle 1 tablespoon parsley over salmon, and top with capers, if desired.

parmesan pecan crusted sticks MAKES 4 SERVINGS

These are the tastiest bread sticks you'll ever dip into a comforting bowl of soup.

4 large eggs

1 cup cream

4 tablespoons honey

6 tablespoons Dijon mustard

1/2 teaspoon salt

1 cup ground or finely chopped pecans

1/2 cup toasted breadcrumbs

1/2 cup grated Parmesan cheese

4 tablespoons dried parsley flakes

8 thick slices day-old firm white bread

Butter

In a pie plate or other shallow pan, whisk together the eggs, cream, honey, mustard, and salt. In another pie plate, mix together the pecans, breadcrumbs, cheese, and parsley. Dip the bread slices in the egg mixture until soaked on each side and then in the nut mixture, pressing firmly, and turning over until completely coated.

Melt a little butter in a small frying pan over medium-high heat. Add 1 coated bread slice to the pan, cover, and cook on each side for about 3 minutes, or until well browned and crisp. Repeat with remaining slices. Cut each slice into 3–4 strips to serve.

desserts

cookie-crusted sundaes MAKES 6 SERVINGS

The cookie crumbs form a sweet and crunchy crust for the French toast slices, making a perfect base for sundae toppings.

- 3 large eggs
- 1 cup half-and-half
- 1 teaspoon vanilla
- 1/2 teaspoon salt
- 6 large snickerdoodle, gingersnap, or sugar cookies
- 6 (1-inch-thick) slices day-old challah or French bread
- 6 scoops ice cream, of choice
- Caramel or chocolate syrup, optional
- Whipped cream, optional
- Chopped nuts, optional
- Maraschino cherries, optional

In a pie plate or other shallow pan, mix together the eggs, half-and-half, vanilla, and salt. Pulse cookies in a food processor to fine crumbs and spread on a plate.

Using cookie cutters, cut bread slices into 4-inch circles or other festive shapes. Dip both sides of each bread shape in egg mixture and then in cookie crumbs.

Heat a small frying pan sprayed with nonstick cooking spray over medium heat. Add 1 coated bread slice to the pan, cover, and cook on each side for 1–2 minutes, or until lightly browned; cool to room temperature. Repeat with remaining slices.

To serve, place each bread shape in an individual bowl or dessert dish with a scoop of ice cream and toppings, as desired.

bread pudding MAKES 6 TO 8 SERVINGS

This marriage of French toast and bread pudding will be love at first bite.

- 8 cups (1-inch cubes) day-old French bread
- 1/4 cup butter, melted
- 4 large eggs plus 2 egg yolks
- 3/4 cup sugar
- 4 cups half-and-half
- 1 tablespoon vanilla
- 1/2 teaspoon salt
- 1/2 teaspoon nutmeg
- 1 cup raisins
- 1/2 cup chopped walnuts
- Whipped cream

Preheat oven to 325 degrees. Prepare a 9 x 13-inch baking pan with nonstick cooking spray.

Spread bread cubes on a baking sheet in a single layer and brush tops with butter. Bake for 10–12 minutes, or until lightly browned; cool to room temperature.

In a bowl, whisk together the eggs, egg yolks, sugar, half-and-half, vanilla, salt, and nutmeg. Toss the bread cubes, raisins, and walnuts in the egg mixture until bread is thoroughly soaked; spread evenly in pan.

Bake, uncovered, for 45–50 minutes, or until browned on top but still slightly jiggly in the center. Let stand 20 minutes before serving, with a dollop of whipped cream on top.

fruit crisp

MAKES 6 TO 8 SERVINGS

French toast crumbles make a great crunchy topping for this traditional dessert.

- 6 large eggs
- 1 cup milk
- 1 teaspoon vanilla
- 1/2 teaspoon salt
- 8 to 10 (1/2-inch-thick) slices day-old challah or French bread
- 2 (21-ounce) cans cherry pie filling
- 1 (20-ounce) can crushed pineapple, with liquid
- 1 cup chopped pecans
- 1/2 cup sugar
- 1 teaspoon cinnamon
- Whipped cream, optional

Preheat oven to 400 degrees.

In a pie plate or other shallow pan, whisk together the eggs, milk, vanilla, and salt. Soak each bread slice in egg mixture for 30 seconds on each side, or until soaked through.

Heat a small frying pan sprayed with nonstick spray over medium-high heat. Add 1 soaked bread slice to the pan, cover, and cook on each side for 2–3 minutes, or until well browned; repeat with remaining bread slices. Cool to room temperature, and then very finely dice. Spread on a baking sheet in a single layer and bake for 10–12 minutes, or until dried and crisp.

In a 3- to 4-quart casserole dish, stir together the pie filling, pineapple and liquid, and pecans. In a bowl, mix together the sugar and cinnamon, add toasted bread, and toss to coat; spread evenly over fruit mixture. Bake for 30–40 minutes, or until cooked through and bubbly on edges. Garnish with whipped cream, if desired.

banana splits MAKES 6 SERVINGS

Fun fact: The banana split was invented in 1904 by a 23-year-old apprentice pharmacist at Tassel's Pharmacy in Latrobe, Pennsylvania. Well over 100 years old, it's time for a makeover.

1 (10-ounce) jar maraschino cherries, drained

8 ounces cream cheese, softened

1/2 cup powdered sugar

3 large eggs

2/3 cup milk

1 teaspoon vanilla

1/2 teaspoon salt

12 (1/2-inch-thick) slices day-old challah or French bread

3 bananas, sliced lengthwise and halved

6 scoops ice cream, of choice

Chocolate syrup

Reserve 6 cherries with stems for garnish, and dice the remaining cherries. In a bowl, mix together the diced cherries, cream cheese, and sugar until well-combined.

In a pie plate or other shallow pan, whisk together the eggs, milk, vanilla, and salt. Dip both sides of each bread slice in egg mixture until just soaked. Heat a small frying pan sprayed with nonstick cooking spray over medium-high heat. Add 1 soaked bread slice to the pan, cover, and cook on both sides for 1–2 minutes, or until lightly browned. Repeat with remaining bread slices. Chill French toast slices 30 minutes, or until cold.

To serve, place 1 slice of French toast in an individual bowl or dessert dish. Layer 1/3 cup cream cheese mixture, 1 banana slice, and another slice of French toast over top. Add 1 scoop of ice cream and drizzle with chocolate syrup; top with a reserved cherry.

chocolate decadence stacks MAKES 6 SERVINGS

This sweet and creamy concoction is a chocolate lover's dream.

1 cup heavy cream, whipped

½ cup sugar

8 ounces whipped cream cheese, room temperature

1 teaspoon vanilla

½ cup plus 1 tablespoon gourmet cocoa powder, divided

3 large eggs

1 cup milk

½ teaspoon salt

12 (½-inch-thick) slices day-old angel food cake

8 ounces dark Swiss chocolate, grated

In a medium bowl, using a hand mixer, mix together the whipped cream, sugar, cream cheese, vanilla, and ½ cup cocoa powder until well-combined; place in the refrigerator to chill.

In a pie plate or other shallow pan, whisk together the eggs, milk, 1 tablespoon cocoa powder, and salt. Soak cake slices in egg mixture for about 30 seconds on each side. Heat a small frying pan sprayed with nonstick cooking spray over medium heat. Add 1 soaked cake slice to the pan, cover, and cook on each side for 2–3 minutes, or until lightly browned; remove and cool to slightly warm. Repeat with remaining cake slices. Toast cooked slices in a toaster and cool to room temperature.

To serve, place 1 cake slice on individual serving plates and spread a thick layer of cream cheese mixture over top. Sprinkle 1 tablespoon grated chocolate over cream cheese and repeat for a second layer.

pudding stuffed toast MAKES 6 SERVINGS

This French toast dessert proves that any dessert is better with rich, creamy pudding in the middle.

4 large eggs

½ cup heavy cream

1 tablespoon cinnamon

¼ cup sugar

1 teaspoon vanilla

½ teaspoon salt

6 (1½-inch-thick) slices day-old French bread

1 (3.4 ounce) box instant pudding mix, any flavor

1½ cups very cold milk

Specialty syrup, of choice (see 116-125)

In a bowl, whisk together the eggs, cream, cinnamon, sugar, vanilla, and salt until frothy. Pour half of the egg mixture into a 9 x 13-inch pan. Place bread slices in pan, completely filling pan. Pour remaining egg mixture evenly over bread and let soak for 20 minutes.

Heat a small frying pan sprayed with nonstick cooking spray over medium-high heat. Add 1 soaked bread slice to the pan, cover, and cook on each side for 2–3 minutes, or until lightly browned. Repeat with remaining bread slices and then chill for 1–2 hours.

In a medium bowl, add the pudding mix and milk and mix together as directed on box. Remove bread from refrigerator and slice lengthwise in half partway through, forming a pocket in the middle. Fill with 2 heaping tablespoons of pudding and serve with a drizzle of syrup over top.

chocolate pistachio sandwiches MAKES 8 SANDWICHES

This decadent dessert yields a yummy surprise when warm chocolate oozes from the first bite.

8 ounces (60 percent cocoa) extra-fine baking chocolate, grated

2 cups heavy cream, divided

½ cup sugar

16 thick slices day-old firm white bread, crusts removed

1 cup ground or very finely chopped pistachios, divided

4 large eggs

1 teaspoon vanilla

½ teaspoon salt

2 cups chocolate wafer cookie crumbs

Chocolate syrup

Place chocolate in a small bowl. In a saucepan, add 1 cup cream and sugar; bring to a boil, stirring, until sugar is dissolved. Pour boiling mixture over chocolate and stir until melted; place in refrigerator to chill for 2 hours, or until firm. Evenly divide and roll the chocolate into 8 balls, and then flatten each one into a ¼- to ½-inch-thick disk. Place the chocolate disks on 8 bread slices; divide and sprinkle ½ cup pistachios evenly over chocolate. Top with remaining bread slices and press lightly to seal.

Preheat oven to 425 degrees. Lightly oil a large baking sheet.

In a pie plate or other shallow pan, whisk together 1 cup cream, eggs, vanilla, and salt. Mix the cookie crumbs together with remaining pistachios and spread on a plate. Dip the sandwiches in the egg mixture and then the crumbs, pressing lightly. Place on baking sheet and bake for 8 minutes; turn sandwiches over and bake 5 minutes more. Serve hot with a drizzle of syrup over top.

lemony blueberry cobbler MAKES 6 TO 8 SERVINGS

All the taste of classic blueberry cobbler in a French toast dish.

6 large eggs

1 cup liquid vanilla coffee creamer

8 cups (1-inch cubes) day-old French bread

6 cups fresh or frozen and thawed blueberries

3 tablespoons cornstarch

1/2 cup sugar

2 tablespoons fresh-squeezed lemon juice

1 teaspoon lemon zest

Whipped cream or ice cream, optional

Preheat oven to 400 degrees.

In a large bowl, whisk together the eggs and creamer. Add bread cubes, tossing until evenly coated; set aside. (Toss with a spoon occasionally to make sure liquid is evenly absorbed.)

In a separate bowl, toss berries with cornstarch, sugar, juice, and zest; place in a 4-quart baking dish, and spread soaked bread cubes evenly over top. Bake, uncovered, for 30–40 minutes, or until cooked through and bubbly around the edges. Serve topped with whipped cream or ice cream, if desired.

VARIATION: *Once mixture is ready to bake, it can be divided into individual ramekins and baked for 30 minutes, or until baked through and bubbly around the edges.*

seven-layer strawberry torte

MAKES 6 TO 8 SERVINGS

This spectacular treat is an easy but elegant twist on everyone's favorite dessert–strawberry shortcake.

- 8 cups sliced fresh strawberries plus 1 whole strawberry
- 1 cup plus 2 tablespoons sugar, divided
- 3 large eggs
- 1 cup milk
- 1/2 teaspoon salt
- 2 teaspoons vanilla, divided
- 6 (8-inch diameter) pita breads
- 2 cups heavy cream

In a bowl, gently stir together the sliced strawberries and 1/2 cup sugar; set aside. In a pie plate or other shallow pan, whisk together the eggs, milk, salt, and 1 teaspoon vanilla. Soak each pita in egg mixture for about 2 minutes, or until softened.

Heat a medium frying pan sprayed with nonstick cooking spray over medium-high heat. Add 1 soaked pita to the pan, cover, and cook on each side for 1–2 minutes, or until lightly browned. Repeat process and cool cooked pitas to room temperature; sprinkle 1 teaspoon of sugar over each pita.

Place the cream, 1 teaspoon vanilla, and 1/2 cup sugar in a large bowl and beat until thick and peaks start to form.

To assemble the torte, place 1 pita in the center of a large round serving platter. Spread 2/3 cup whipped cream evenly over the top and arrange 1 cup sliced strawberries over the cream. Repeat layers ending with whipped cream and the whole strawberry on top to garnish. Refrigerate 1 hour before serving.

crème brûlée style french toast MAKES 6 TOASTS

This twist on an elegant French dessert serves up that classic caramelized sugar-crusted flavor everyone loves.

- 1/4 cup butter
- 1/2 cup brown sugar
- 2 tablespoons corn syrup
- 6 (1 1/2-inch-thick) slices day-old challah bread
- 5 large eggs
- 1 1/2 cups heavy cream
- 1 tablespoon vanilla
- 1/2 teaspoon salt
- 6 tablespoons sugar

Melt butter in a small frying pan over medium heat. Stir in brown sugar and syrup and cook, stirring constantly, until sugar is dissolved. Pour mixture into a 9 x 13-inch baking pan and arrange bread slices on top.

In a bowl, whisk together the eggs, cream, vanilla, and salt. Pour egg mixture over the bread slices, making sure to saturate completely. Cover and refrigerate at least 2 hours or overnight. Remove from refrigerator and bring to room temperature, about 30 minutes.

Preheat oven to 375 degrees.

Bake, uncovered, for 40–45 minutes, or until puffed and lightly browned. To serve, place each slice on an individual serving plate and sprinkle 1 tablespoon sugar evenly over top. Using a kitchen torch, melt the sugar until caramelized and crisp.

NOTE: *If you don't have a kitchen torch, broil on high for about 2 minutes, until caramelized and crisp, watching carefully so as not to burn.*

specialty syrups and sauces

maple cream syrup MAKES 2 CUPS

1 cup sugar

½ cup butter

½ cup pure maple syrup

¼ cup milk or cream

In a small saucepan, bring to a simmer the sugar, butter, syrup, and milk or cream. Simmer, stirring frequently, until sugar is dissolved and syrup is slightly thickened. Serve warm. Store in the refrigerator for up to 2 weeks.

decadent vanilla cream syrup MAKES 2 CUPS

1 cup cream

½ cup sugar

1 tablespoon flour

4 egg yolks

1 tablespoon vanilla

1 cup vanilla ice cream

In a small saucepan, bring the cream and sugar to a boil over medium-high heat, stirring constantly.

In a small bowl, mix together the flour, egg yolks, and vanilla. Stir a few spoonfuls of the boiling cream mixture into the egg yolk mixture, and then pour the tempered egg yolk mixture into the cream mixture, stirring constantly for 3 minutes. Add the ice cream and continue to cook for another 3 minutes, stirring constantly until thickened. Serve warm. Store in the refrigerator for up to 2 weeks.

blueberry syrup MAKES 2 CUPS

1 cup sugar

½ cup corn syrup

1 cup blueberries

1 teaspoon vanilla

In a blender, add the sugar, syrup, and blueberries and blend until smooth. Pour into a small saucepan and bring to a simmer, stirring for 3 minutes. Remove from heat and cool for 5 minutes. Stir in vanilla. Serve warm. Store in the refrigerator for up to 2 weeks.

raspberry syrup MAKES 3 CUPS

1 (12-ounce) container frozen apple raspberry juice concentrate, thawed

3 tablespoons cornstarch

2 cups fresh or frozen raspberries, thawed

In a medium saucepan, mix together the juice and cornstarch; bring to a simmer, stirring until thickened. Remove from heat and stir in raspberries. Serve warm. Store in the refrigerator for up to 2 weeks.

cranapple compote MAKES 3 CUPS

½ cup butter

3 Golden Delicious apples, peeled and diced

1 cup chopped fresh cranberries

½ cup sugar

1 (12-ounce) container frozen apple juice concentrate, thawed

¼ cup corn syrup

2 tablespoons brown sugar

In a medium saucepan over medium-high heat, melt the butter and sauté apples for 2 minutes. Add the cranberries and sugar and stir until cranberries pop, about 2 minutes more. Stir in juice, syrup, and brown sugar. Simmer, stirring frequently, until thickened and sugar has dissolved, about 5 minutes. Remove from heat and cool slightly before serving. Store in the refrigerator for up to 2 weeks.

chunky cherry syrup MAKES ABOUT 3 CUPS

1 (14-ounce) can sour pitted cherries, drained and chopped

1 cup corn syrup

½ cup sugar

Red food coloring, optional

Place cherries in a small saucepan. Add syrup and sugar and bring to a full rolling boil. Reduce heat and let simmer for 25–30 minutes, or until thickened, stirring occasionally. Turn off heat and add a few drops of food coloring, if desired. Let cool to warm and serve. Store in the refrigerator for up to 2 weeks.

fresh fruit purée MAKES 2 CUPS

3 cups fresh fruit or berries, of choice

1 teaspoon lemon juice

2 tablespoons pure maple syrup

2 tablespoons light corn syrup

Water

In a blender, add the fruit, lemon juice, maple syrup, and corn syrup; blend together, adding water 1 tablespoon at a time, if necessary, to desired syrup consistency. Store in the refrigerator for up to 1 week.

easy blender hollandaise sauce MAKES ABOUT 1 CUP

3 egg yolks

1 tablespoon lemon juice

1/4 teaspoon salt

1/4 teaspoon white pepper

1/2 cup butter

In a blender, add the egg yolks, lemon juice, salt, and pepper; blend to combine. Place butter in a microwave-safe bowl, and melt in microwave until sizzling hot. Turn blender on low and slowly pour in the melted butter until combined. Serve warm. Store in the refrigerator for 3–5 days.

cinnamon cream syrup MAKES ABOUT 1 ½ CUPS

1 cup sugar

½ cup corn syrup

½ teaspoon cinnamon

½ cup evaporated milk

In a small saucepan, combine sugar, syrup, and cinnamon. Bring to a boil, stirring for 3 minutes. Remove from heat and cool for 5 minutes. Stir in milk to combine. Serve warm. Store in the refrigerator for up to 1 week.

old-fashioned buttermilk syrup MAKES 2 CUPS

½ cup butter

1 ½ cups sugar

2 tablespoons light corn syrup

¾ cup buttermilk

2 teaspoons vanilla

1 teaspoon baking soda

Melt the butter in a small saucepan over medium heat; stir in remaining ingredients. Reduce heat to medium-low and bring to a simmer. Cook, stirring frequently for 7–8 minutes, until slightly thickened. Serve warm. Store in the refrigerator for up to 2 weeks.

citrus sunshine syrup MAKES ABOUT 2 CUPS

2 tablespoons sugar

1 tablespoon lemon zest

2 tablespoons orange zest

1 1/2 cups corn syrup

2 tablespoons frozen orange juice concentrate, thawed

2 tablespoons lemon juice

1 cinnamon stick

In a small bowl mix sugar and zests together; let stand at least 30 minutes. Place in a blender and add remaining ingredients except cinnamon; blend until smooth, about 1 minute.

Pour mixture into a small saucepan and bring to a simmer over medium heat; add the cinnamon stick and simmer for about 20 minutes, until slightly thickened, stirring every 2 minutes. Remove and discard cinnamon stick before serving. Store in the refrigerator for up to 2 weeks.

index

METRIC CONVERSION CHART

Volume Measurements		Weight Measurements		Temperature Conversion	
U.S.	Metric	U.S.	Metric	Fahrenheit	Celsius
1 teaspoon	5 ml	1/2 ounce	15 g	250	120
1 tablespoon	15 ml	1 ounce	30 g	300	150
1/4 cup	60 ml	3 ounces	90 g	325	160
1/3 cup	75 ml	4 ounces	115 g	350	180
1/2 cup	125 ml	8 ounces	225 g	375	190
2/3 cup	150 ml	12 ounces	350 g	400	200
3/4 cup	175 ml	1 pound	450 g	425	220
1 cup	250 ml	2 1/4 pounds	1 kg	450	230

Whisk eggs & MILK

Whisk eggs & MILK